Written by: Joseph Brown

Editor: LaShonda C. Henderson

ISBN-13: **978-1-7321319-5-8**

Published by: Cshantay Publishing

A family that plans together, grows together, thriving is an intentional act.
~LaShonda C. Henderson

# Contents

# Parental Reaction

## Building, Maintaining, and Restructuring Family Bonds

# Introduction

This book began as a school project for an International Baccalaureate (IB), Creativity Activity and Service (CAS) project. The IB program looks for opportunities to intrigue inquiring minds., and give back to the community.

Parenting is very hard, many say there is no real way to teach how to parent, so we wrote this book as a milestone to guide parents on effectively interacting with their children.

# Infant to Child

# Chapter 1: Education

Children in this range are 0 to 5 years of age. According to United States Health and Human Services, infants perform the following milestones, "Copies some movements and facial expressions, like smiling or frowning" while a 5 Year old is indicated as, "More likely to agree with rules" (Services, 2020).

It is common knowledge that infancy is when children learn the fastest. It is also when they are most impressionable. This stage of learning requires that a child study you the most! They are watching your every facial expression, movement, manner of speech and reproducing your behavior. They are gullible and seek to please. In this stage, ALL members of the family must be deliberate with their actions and aware of the consequences that will display in the behavior of their little one.

Reading is one of the greatest education tools. Even though for most of this period, they can't read for themselves, they still benefit greatly from being told stories. We have broken out the age groups because we understand the speed of learning during these years, it is important to note the difference in the age range. All ages require access to use their imagination to make sense of the world, because they are STILL learning their new bodies and minds.

Age 0-At this age the infant doesn't understand the story line. What is most important is the sound of the parent's voice. The baby will begin to mimic sounds, so stories provide a rhythm, and a speech pattern. Replication is the key here. You want stories that are simple. This means small words and engaging activities. For example, a story that my Mom would read to me is "Go dog Go" by P.D. Eastman, another is "The Giving Tree" by Shell Silverstein. These books have simple language and a strong moral basis.

Age 1- Similarly to year 0 the reading technique is the same. The stories are repeated and the toddler looks on curiosity. There is no change in the book type, however you should begin slowly introducing need words so that your child will be able to communicate these needs to you more effectively which reduces temper tantrums.

Age 2- This year you see a repeat in the same types of books and interaction. This year does see one change.

An introduction of interactive books, things to expand their sense of touch, and sound. These types of books expand the expressive words that the child has access to.

Age 3- At this age, your child is should have basic learning and should be decent at speech, but they want to learn the world with their own hands, keep an eye on them as they wander, keep toys, and books the child shows interest in at hands reach for the child.

Age 4- 4-year-olds like new things, those old books you have are not going to be the end. You need to find new yet safe mediums to entertain them with learning, this will be discussed in media and interaction.

Age 5 They are climbers, “out of reach” is less of a problem and what will they do to get something in reach is the issue. They still want to learn about the world but a 5-year-old can be reasoned with, use this to teach lessons about compromise and consequences, verbally.

Media

When you’re dealing with an infant or small toddler you have to make sure you watch what they consume, vet the media you expose them to. If they want to try a game, beat it yourself first, they want to watch a movie watch it yourself first, same with books, and tv shows so that you may truly understand and warn against medias that may be harmful.

Interaction

These kids are mischievous watch them closely. They also at this point need lots of social interaction so be on guard for them to come crashing in when you don't want them to.

# Chapter 2 Finances

## Budgeting

You must have a plan. Small children are prone to accidents, and if you do not have a reserve fund, then high stress can show itself in how you treat your child. Children do not make money, but they have all types of cleaver methods to help you spend it. Consider the clothing you buy; do you need named brands? Can you find clean, comfortable, and affordable items that will not break your bank?

Previously we discussed home education, but part of the budget process is considering what sort of formal education you are willing to pay for these age ranges. Will you seek a daycare or begin early head start private or public programs?

Homebuying

Ensure that you have a stable home environment. You may not be in a space to afford to buy a home, but you should begin to put yourself in a position to. This means, look for opportunities to reduce costs and save money for a down payment.

Strategic Planning- Set college funding. Most states have a college fund that you can pay in monthly or yearly. Starting early, ensures that college will not be a costly endeavor. You want to plan and have a long-range method of paying to further your child's future.

# Chapter 3 Mission

## Standard Operating Procedures

Parents should demonstrate the virtue of talking and understanding the cause behind issues rather than physical punishing. Studies have proven that positive reinforcement is a much better form of correction. And leaves fewer adverse side effects.

The way the household functions will be exhibited by a five year old at kindergarten, if you solve all situations by yelling at home, then your child will yell at others, do as I say, and as I do. If you use physical abuse rather than instructing communication, then your child will display violence as violence is now seen as the solution to disliked behaviors. Just as you are a person with feelings, your child is one too, we aren't all knowing so explanations go a long way towards a healthier and calmer relationship between parent and child.

## Mission Statement

Your mission statement should be the goal that you develop to guide all decisions in a household no matter what topic is at hand. An example of a mission statement is this, "To create a household that leads to the building of a strong and emotionally stable child."

## Decision Strategy

Children at that this age need to learn how to choose small parts of their life. This includes what they eat, color of clothing, and other choices that are none life threatening. This allows the child to begin a healthy thought pattern and teaches how to make decisions on their own.

# Chapter 4 Risks

## Internal

Environment risks include household set up. Baby proof your home. Children at this age are curios and are prone to self-harm as they learn their bodies and the world around them.

## External

Make sure you lock doors are locked so they open the front door and go exploring outside on their own.

# Chapter 5 Setbacks

## Negative Reinforcement

SPANKING is pain-based punishment and it is illegal. It is proven to be ineffective and teaches violence and discourages communication. If you yell, your child yell. Monitor your volume level and tone ensure that loud talking is to alert for danger and not a method belittling the child.

## Positive Reinforcement

The method of redirection allows for children to be guided away from dangers and scenarios that may cause harm. Gentle words, clear communication and rewards to reinforce good behavior.

# Chapter 6 Communication

Style

Children are people too, they deserve to be treated with a level of respect and equality. Parenting is a relationship and if you want to build a strong relationship you need to have a level of respect and trust. Explaining things to your children and treating them like people allows for you to more easily build a relationship as they can understand and respect your decisions more as they understand your train of thought.

**Purpose**

Consider what you want to communicate , as you change how you speak based on your purpose remember that they are always watching you, use simple yet appropriate language based on what you want to do and what you want your child to do. Because I said so is not going to get you far as you deal with older kids an appropriate reason and logic behind your word will let you have higher obedience and cooperation

# Chapter 7 Leisure

**How does your family have fun?**

Consider the music videos and other media consumed consider vetting media before exposing them to the media. If they want to play a game that is single player beat it yourself first so you know the content, if they want to play a multiplayer game play a few rounds before determining its quality. The human bodies is an organic machine, it will degrade if ti is not properly used. This is especially important to have children move around and be outside. The body requires the influence of the sun in order to produce some biochemicals necessary for function. Melanin is  a chemical that resists the sun to prevent sunburn and produce vitamins, despite the resistance to the sun small children have a much more sensitive and weak skin and sunscreen is a good safety tool even black people can get sunburns despite them being less likely.

# Child to Teen

As of now you have the basics for the early stage of life which while most energetic is also the most uniform, past this point you must build plans of your own to raise your child not anyone else's child. Consider who your child is and help engage them to determine your future.

# Chapter 1: Education

## Reading

## Media

## Interaction

# Chapter 2 Finances

## Budgeting

## Homebuying

## Strategic Planning

# Chapter 3 Mission

## Standard Operating Procedures

## Mission Statement

## Decision Strategy

Joseph J. Brown

# Chapter 4 Risks

Internal

External

# Chapter 5 Setbacks

## Negative Reinforcement

## Positive Reinforcement

## Opportunities for Growth

# Chapter 6 Communication

## Style

## Purpose

## Intended Outcome

# Chapter 7 Leisure

How does your family have fun

## Harmful Methods

## Helpful Methods

# Teen to Adult

# Chapter 1: Education

## Reading

# Media

## Interaction

## Budgeting

## Homebuying

## Strategic Planning

## Chapter 3 Mission

# Standard Operating Procedures

## Mission Statement

## Decision Strategy

# Chapter 4 Risks

## Internal

External

# Chapter 5 Setbacks

## Negative Reinforcement

## Positive Reinforcement

Opportunities for Growth

# Chapter 6 Communication Style

## Purpose

Intended Outcome

## Chapter 7 Leisure

How does your family have fun?

## Harmful Methods

## Helpful Methods

www.ingramcontent.com/pod-product-compliance
Lightning Source LLC
LaVergne TN
LVHW020658100826
845148LV00012B/2551